A Simple Guide To Completing Strength-Based Assessments in Adult Social Care

Author Profile:
Email: thesecretsocialworker@yahoo.com

Copyright © 2020 The Secret Social Worker

Disclaimer

No part of this book may be reproduced or used in any manner without written permission of the copyright owner.

Although the author and publisher have made every effort to ensure that the information in this book was correct at press time, the author and publisher do not assume and hereby disclaim any liability to any party for any loss, damage, or disruption caused by errors or omissions, whether such errors or omissions result from negligence, accident, or any other cause.

Introduction

Social work is a complex and challenging career for anyone deciding to take the plunge. It is also the most rewarding and emotionally driven role that no one can quite prepare you for.

There are many individuals working within adult social care, whose roles are to complete simple needs assessments, providing simple support such as adaptations, reablement services as well as researching other organisations and services that could support individuals to maintain their independence as well as overall health and wellbeing.

These workers do not receive the same level of training as many social workers and can face daunting tasks, including having challenging conversations with individuals and their families in need of support.

This simple guide to strength-based assessments has been completed with unqualified workers in mind to assist their understanding in a clear and concise way. The aim is to build confidence and ensure the best level of support to individuals accessing adult social care.

This booklet may also be useful to social work students whilst on placement as well as professionals who want a simple refresher to aid them in their work.

As I always like to stress, This is not a definitive guide. The conversation you have during an assessment is very much dependent on your professional judgements as well as the individuals views and wishes.

About Me

I have been a qualified social worker since 2015 although I have worked within adult social care for over 10 years. I have worked in an out of hours social work team known as the Emergency Duty Team, a learning disability team, initial contact team (including hospital admissions and new community referrals) as well as more recently a long term adults team.

I have recently taken a break from social work to focus on my family as well as my own wellbeing. As a social worker, our own mental health is too easy to forget and push to the side. This time away has reignited my passion for my chosen career and has given me the time as well as confidence to write in a field I am passionate about.

I have decided not to use my real name for the sake of my own mental health. I hope you understand and appreciate my wish to remain anonymous in this way.

I thank you for taking the time to read my book and would greatly appreciate it if you could write a review at the end. It only needs to be a few words and will greatly help me in my future work.

Table of Contents

Disclaimer

Introduction

About Me

Table of Contents

What does strength-based mean?

Preparing for a strength-based assessment

The Assessment

Example of a simple, strength-based assessment

Carers

Conclusion

What does strength-based mean?

'Strength-based' is a term used in social work practice to refer to an individual's self-determination and assets to assist them in achieving their goals as well as reaching their full potential. The aim of this approach is to enable and empower an individual to be as independent as possible in a meaningful and supportive way. A strength based assessment/support plan will have the following attributes:

- **Person centred** - This means that the individual is the expert of their own lives, with focus paid to their understanding of their situation as well as their perceived strengths and skills. The assessment and support will be focussed on the individual, their goals and how they feel they can achieve these.
- **Collaborative working** - It will be clear who is currently involved in the individuals care and support, including how they are currently assisting the individual as well as the length of time this will be for. Roles will be clearly defined and understood by all involved to ensure a successful outcome for the individual.
- **Meaningful choices** - The individuals voice will be heard throughout the assessment (person-centered) with their choices clearly expressed following the appropriate information being provided to them to enable the individual to make an informed decision. Any decisions that could be

seen as 'unwise' will have been clearly outlined with a rationale behind this. This is providing there is no concerns around the individuals capacity to make informed decisions about their lives.
- **Effective Communication** - This will be evidenced within the assessment with there being a detailed understanding of the individual, their needs, goals and support in place or to be put in place to assist them in achieving these.

Preparing for a strength-based assessment

It can be tempting to rush into an assessment when there are deadlines and a large list of people requiring support. However, by rushing into an assessment, information can often be missed and there is a high probability of there being a delay in any support required. This can have a significant impact on the individual and all those involved in that persons care and support. To ensure a positive and strength-based assessment that is focused on the person, the following considerations should be made:

- **Read the referral** - It is important to ensure a full understanding of the referral and what is being requested of you as a worker. Making your own notes and writing down any further questions you have to ensure you are clear on the situation. For example, hospital assessments tend to have a lot of jargon that at times can be difficult to understand. Make sure you contact the ward staff and clarify this to ensure the individual is getting the right worker from the start.
- **Contact the referrer** - This is such an important step in the assessment process. It enables you to get a clearer snapshot of the potential situation and possible needs. As well as this it is where you can clarify whether **consent** has been obtained by the

referrer from the individual the assessment is being requested for. If consent has not been given by the individual you may wish to consider the appropriateness of the referral and what steps should be taken next. This is something you would discuss with your manager.
- **Capacity** - Always ask whether the individual being referred understands why this is and what it means for them moving forwards. throughout. Remember, if an individual has capacity, the decision to complete a needs assessment is in their control. If there are concerns in regards to the individuals capacity, note down why and discuss with management. A qualified social worker may be best placed to take on this case.
- **Hospital assessments** - If the referral is an assessment notification from a hospital, it will be appropriate to enquire as to what treatment and support they have provided the individual since their admission. For example, have they been seen by the physiotherapist and occupational therapist? Have they been seen by the hospital mental health team where appropriate? What aids have they been using on the ward and what tasks have they required support with any why? What will they be returning home with? Has an assessment of the home been carried out if appropriate by the occupational therapist to ensure it's safe to return to? What was the reason for admission and any diagnoses relevant to the referral? When is the

estimated discharge date? What are the last notes from the consultant in charge? Has consent been obtained and what does the person feel they will require upon discharge? **All this information will help in considering possible support before completing the assessment and will also be useful if you are wishing to discuss the case with your manager. Again, it may be found from this information that the case would be appropriate for a social worker and could save you time as well as preventing a change in worker for the person. They likely already feel very nervous and vulnerable.**

- **Make contact -** Once I have completed the above steps I will contact the individual the referral has been made for or an appropriate person where required (family member etc). I will go through the referral with them for their information and to ensure my understanding of their situation in their view as well as the urgency of the assessment. I also find this a good time to outline the assessment process. Depending on the situation and the urgency, a face to face discussion about this may be best however. Speak to your manager to ensure you have taken the correct steps if you are unsure. If there is enough time, send a letter with the individuals assessment date and time to them and any other attendees that have been agreed upon. It may also be appropriate to send further information on the reablement process and the assessment process where possible. By doing this you are working to achieve a good working relationship as well as setting clear expectations, which can support more difficult conversations that may be needed in the future.

- **Other professional involvements** - Some individuals may have significant health diagnoses with various specialists involved. These can include psychiatrists, specialist nurses, General Practitioners, Occupational therapists as well as care home managers and support staff. Although it may not be appropriate for everyone to be involved, it may be beneficial to make contact and gather further information from them as this will help towards the overall assessment and any support required. Always seek consent from the individual where possible prior to having these discussions.

The Assessment

Once you have completed the previous actions, you will hopefully be ready to commence the assessment with an idea of where the focus needs to be and the possible outcomes, including the desired outcomes of the individual. Obviously this is not always the case and situations can be very different upon your arrival.

Prior to commencing the assessment, discuss what your role is and what kind of support you can potentially offer to the individual and their family/carers. Discuss the reablement process if you feel this may become an appropriate avenue and ensure there is a clear understanding of your role. Providing this information at the start of the assessment will ensure an honest and transparent approach to individuals assessment and any future support they receive. This will also assist in developing a strong working relationship with them.

When completing a strength based assessment, it is important consider the following factors when discussing each area (for example, Health and wellbeing, communication etc):

- What are the individual strengths? What do they feel they can do and what were they able to do prior to their current situation?

- What are their current abilities? What do they feel they are able to manage in their current circumstances?
- What aids/support to they currently have in place and is this a long term arrangement?
- What is the individual hoping to achieve? Where do they see themselves in 6 weeks/6 months/1 year?
- Given the above, what support can be offered that can assist the individual to reach their goals and improve their level of independence as well as overall health and wellbeing? - consider aids and adaptations, reablement, voluntary organisations, family, friends, community, other professions such as district nurses and so on.

Top Tip: It is important that you ensure a good understanding of what is available in the local community. Take time to research possible services in the area that could benefit the people you work with. For example: Alzheimer's Society, Carers Association etc. These services provide vital support, information and activities that can make a significant and positive difference to an individuals quality of life.

Example of a simple, strength-based assessment

To support you in achieving a proportionate strength-based assessment that is focused on the individual, an example has been written below. Please remember every assessment in unique and always depends on what the individual wishes to share. Please remember this is their assessment and should always be meaningful and relevant to them. This is a simple example and should not be copied.

Individual summary: Elsie is a 94 year old lady who has lived in her village for 70 years following her marriage to her late husband, Brian. Elsie has advised that brian was a builder and built their bungalow from scratch. This is a very important place for Elsie, with it being where all her children were born and raised as well as where Brian passed away four years ago at the age of 92.

Elsie has always been a very active lady, enjoying fell walks with the local walkers club up until the age of 78. Since then, Elsie has been going for leisurely walks a few times a week with friends from the walking club. Elsie has said this brings her a lot of joy as she can become lonely at times with her son, Thomas and daughter, Paula living in London.

Elsie experienced a fall whilst trying to get out of the bath a few days ago. Elsie, along with ward staff have advised that she has experienced three falls in the last two weeks for the same reason. Elsie has some significant bruising to her left hip, which she says is uncomfortable to walk on at present although has not broken any bones.

Elsie is determined to be as independent as possible although she is feeling very anxious about her mobility following the fall and the subsequent bruising. Elsie's current goal is to build her confidence and continue her weekly walks with friends. Elsie's long term goal is to remain in her own home for as long as possible.

Elsie is currently at Darlington memorial Hospital where she has been for two days. Given Elsie's minimal injuries following the fall, the consultant feels Elsie will be able to better recuperate at home in her own environment.

Health and wellbeing: Elsie is generally a very fit and healthy woman and credits this to her healthy lifestyle which includes frequent walking.

Elsie does have high blood pressure which she does take medication for and has advised that she does this independently. The ward staff have advised that Elsie will alert them to when she requires her medication as she likes to take these at certain times of the day. Elsie has advised she enjoys a routine and has tried to maintain this as much as possible during her hospital stay.

When at home, Elsie's medication is delivered by the pharmacy as required. Elsie also has supportive neighbours who transport her to any health appointments at her own request. Elsie is very conscious of her health and has advised that she ensures she attends all appointments necessary. Elsie has advised that I can contact her local GP for more information if required.

Elsie's mobility prior to her falls over the last few weeks is generally good with her able to walk around her village and the surrounding areas at a leisurely pace. Elsie has advised that she does feel more unsteady in the evening however as she likes to be as active as possible during the day.

At present, Elsie is using a zimmer frame to mobilise around the ward. Elsie has advised she does not like using an aid but understands this is an essential part of her recuperation. An occupational therapist from the ward has completed a home visit and has suggested to Elsie that she has a grab rail in her bathroom as well as a bath board to assist her with bathing in the future. Elsie has agreed to this. Elsie will also be taking the zimmer frame home with her with the hope she will progress to a stick in the near future. Elsie has agreed to be referred to the community occupational therapy team, who will provide further support once she is home.

Communication: Elsie has excellent verbal communication and has been able to voice her opinions throughout the assessment with ease.

Elsie wears hearing aids in both her ears and is able to manage these independently. Elsie has a few neighbours who support her with this such as collecting new batteries.

Elsie does wear glasses for reading and is able to write although advises that she tends to send emails and text her friends and family rather than writing letters.

Eating and drinking: Elsie has advised that prior to her fall, she was making her own meals from scratch. Elsie's friend and neighbour, Doreen brought her a sunday roast once a week which she enjoys and has advised she also goes for lunch once a week at least with friends. Elsie enjoys a glass of wine in the evening although she advises she just has one small glass of red wine as this was Brian's favourite.

Elsie has her food shopping delivered and used her laptop to do this. Elsie has advised that she has a saved list which she re-orders most weeks to make it easier. Elsie doesn't enjoy food shopping and finds this method much easier. Elsie's neighbours also ask her regularly if she needs anything.

Elsie has completed a kitchen assessment with the ward occupational therapist (OT). The OT has advised that Elsie was very nervous of her abilities due to the pain in her hip and became shaky when trying to make a cup of tea. Elsie has advised that she was overcome with nerves due to the decline in her confidence. The OT has ordered a perching stool to assist Else upon her return home.

It is very important to Elsie that she can continue to make her own meals as she enjoys the process. Elsie has also advised that it passes the time away with her enjoying baking and cooking a hot meal at lunch time. Elsie prefers cold meals for breakfast and dinner however. Elsie has advised that she would benefit from support to increase her confidence as she does not wish to rely on others long term. Elsie has advised she does not wish for meals on wheels services and would very much prefer not to eat microwave meals.

Personal Care: Elsie has advised that prior to her fall, she was independent in washing and dressing. Elsie has informed me that she did these tasks slowly as they can tire her out at times, however it is important to Elsie that she can maintain her independence in this area.

Whilst in hospital, Elsie has been having a shower with the use of a shower chair. Elsie is able to manage washing and dressing her top half and has required some support with her lower half such as pulling up her stockings.

A home visit has been completed with Elsie's consent by the occupational therapist, who has suggested a grab rail and bath board for Elsie's bathroom. Elsie has agreed to these being ordered and has advised she will not be using her bath until these have arrived.

Elsie has advised that she would like support with washing and dressing in the morning. Elsie feels that she will be able to manage this independently within a short period however. Elsie has also advised that she is scared to use her bath at present and would benefit from having someone with her when taking her first bath for some reassurance.

Running and maintaining the home: Elsie has advised that she always makes her own bed in the morning and does light cleaning around the home such as, cleaning surfaces and dusting.

Elsie has a cleaner who she has used for many years now called Claire. Claire visits twice weekly to clean as well as taking ironing home with her. Elsie would like to continue her own tasks as much as possible when she returns home and feels that with some initial support these should be manageable.

Organising and Managing own life: Elsie has a current account where her pension from her career as a teacher and other benefits are deposited too. Elsie managed these independently. Elsie's daughter, Paula has organised her bills to be paid via direct debit, which Elsie finds much easier. Elsie has advised that she does have a lot in savings that her daughter supports her with if needed. Elsie has advised that she wanted to make sure she has enough to pay for any care in the future if needed as she doesn't want to be a burden on her family and friends.

Leisure: Elsie has been a lover of walking all her life with her trekking all over the world to take part in various walks. This includes visiting Australia, New Zealand and South America. Elsie is unable to walk to the same pace and distance as a result of older age although she continues to go walking twice weekly with friends from her walking group. This is something Elsie is determined to pursue again once she has recovered from her fall.

Elsie accesses the village hall once weekly for her crochet group as well as attending the monthly Bingo trip where she and other 65+ adults catch a bus to the local Bingo night. Elsie also enjoys eating out regularly and often visits friends and has visitors herself. Elsie's children visit three to four times a year each with their children and partners.

Elsie has advised she doesn't enjoy the feeling of loneliness and so tries to do as much as she can to occupy her mind. Elsie feels she is living a meaningful life as a result and enjoys her social life. Elsie has advised that she does still miss her husband, Brian greatly although feels he would be proud of her winnings from Bingo.

Elsie does not feel she requires further assistance in this area although would welcome any suggestions on services or groups that she may enjoy.

Work: Elsie is a retired teacher where she taught primary in her local community. Elsie has volunteered in the past although is not looking for any opportunities at present.

Risk Management: Elsie has telecare in place and wears her pendent on her wrist. Elsie pressed this as appropriate when she fell. This goes straight to the call center at Elsie's request as she doesn't want to burden her neighbours as well as Thomas and Paula living down south in london. Elsie finds this effective in maintaining her safety.

Elsie is aware of how to manage her general safety in regards to a possible fire and does not wish for further information at this time.

Managing own actions: Elsie is very independent and is able to manage her actions appropriately. There have been no issues raised by Elsie or others in this area.

Carers: Elsie has advised that she does not have regular support from others. Eslie's friend, Doreen makes a weekly meal which she has done for many years as well as being one of the many friends and neighbours who support with health appointments when these arise from time to time.

Assessment summary: Elsie is a very determined and independent woman who enjoys being as active as possible.
Elsie has many friends and neighbours who offer support when required although Elsie likes to be as independent as possible with her daily living.

Elsie has experienced a fall which has caused some short term pain to her left hip. Elsie can walk with the use of a zimmer frame although struggles to stand and mobilise independently.

Elsie feels her confidence has depleted as a result of the fall whilst getting out of her bath and is very anxious about returning home although it is her goal to return here and regain her independence following her discharge.

The occupational therapist has completed a home visit and has ordered the following equipment with Elsie's consent:

- Grab rail for bathroom
- Bath board
- Perching stool for kitchen
- Zimmer frame - Elsie has this and will return home with it.

The reablement team has been discussed with Elsie and she feels she will benefit greatly from this short term support to increase her independence and overall confidence. It has been discussed that Elsie would like the following support:

- Support with washing and dressing on a morning
- Support with preparing meals
- Support with first bath when home
- Support and encouragement with mobility around the home

Elsie will have regular input from the community occupational therapist once home as well as her GP making a home visit within the first week she returns. Elsie's medication now includes some pain relief, which she will use as and when required.

Elsie has been provided with information on the reablement service as well as written information on charges should long term support be required. Elsie's daughter, Paula will be collecting her form the hospital and staying with her for two nights for reassurance and initial support. Elsie is keen to get back to her usual routine however and regain her independence.

Carers

Unpaid carers are vital in Adult social care. Without their support, the extra strain on the government to provide care and support to all those that require it would be astronomical. I never really feel that there is enough emphasis on the value of carers within social care and although I don't have any fancy statistics to hand, I'm pretty sure that without these selfless and devoted individuals, the care system would reach breaking point. This is why it is so vital to acknowledge any carers such as family, friends and neighbours. To ensure they have access to the support they need to maintain their caring role as well as having all the information they need should they begin to struggle. Too many carers reach out for support when they have reached crisis point because they were so unsure and worried about how to access support as well as feeling that they may not get any at all.

- **Carers providing support** - Does the individual have anybody providing unpaid support on a regular basis. This could be with meal preparation on a daily basis, managing the home, supporting with personal care twice a day and so on. Is that carer involved in the assessment and do they wish for a carers assessment? If not can they be contacted separately?
- **Carers wellbeing** - Does the carer feel like they are managing in their current role and do they feel

this can be sustained long term? Do they feel they are in need of regular breaks to continue or is there anything they feel would support them further in their role to maintain their carer relationship with the individual?
- **Carers assessment** - Has the carer been offered an assessment in respect of their caring role and what has their response to this been? Have they been sent information on what it entails to ensure their understanding or have they declined involvement? If so it would be beneficial to understand why in the event this could lead to a crisis situation in the future.
- **Information for carers** - Is the carer aware of local carer support groups as well as support groups for specific diagnoses such as Parkinson's and Dementia where they can seek support from other individuals in their situation as well as understanding more about the individual they are caring for?
- **Carers view** - What is the carers view of the individuals current situation and what support do they feel the individual will benefit from? This is dependent on consent being sought from the individual where appropriate to discuss.

Conclusion

As you have read above, strength-based assessments are focused on the person and ensure they are in control of their own assessment. The point of this approach is to consider the person's individual strengths, including the current support network they have around them to enable them to achieve their goals.

The Care Act 2014 has required that local authorities adapt the strength-based approach when carrying out assessments. You can find further information on both the Care Act 2014 and the strength-based approach in social work on **Scie.org.uk.** You may also wish to purchase my in-depth book: **'Social Work Assessments in Adult Social Care: Considerations to Make When Undertaking Needs Assessments.**

If you are ever in doubt always refer to your manager for support and ensure you use information available to you in your workplace to ensure you are following the correct policies and guidelines.

Printed in Great Britain
by Amazon